D1327481

Matter Close-Up

What is a gas?

by Lynn Peppas

Crabtree Publishing Company

www.crabtreebooks.com

Author
Lynn Peppas

**Publishing plan research
and development**
Sean Charlebois, Reagan Miller
Crabtree Publishing Company

Editor
Kathy Middleton

Proofreader
Wendy Scavuzzo

Photo research and graphic design
Katherine Berti

Print and production coordinator
Katherine Berti

Photographs by Shutterstock and Thinkstock

Library and Archives Canada Cataloguing in Publication

Peppas, Lynn
        What is a gas? / Lynn Peppas.

(Matter close-up)
Includes index.
Issued also in electronic format.
ISBN 978-0-7787-0769-1 (bound).--ISBN 978-0-7787-0776-9 (pbk.)

        1. Gases--Juvenile literature. I. Title. II. Series: Matter close-up

QC161.2.P47 2012   j530.4'3   C2012-904361-3

Library of Congress Cataloging-in-Publication Data

CIP available at Library of Congress

Crabtree Publishing Company

www.crabtreebooks.com   1-800-387-7650

Printed in Hong Kong/092012/BK20120629

Published in Canada
Crabtree Publishing
616 Welland Ave.
St. Catharines, Ontario
L2M 5V6

Published in the United States
Crabtree Publishing
PMB 59051
350 Fifth Avenue, 59th Floor
New York, New York 10118

Published in the United Kingdom
Crabtree Publishing
Maritime House
Basin Road North, Hove
BN41 1WR

Published in Australia
Crabtree Publishing
3 Charles Street
Coburg North
VIC 3058

Contents

What is the matter?

Matter is all around you. Matter is anything that takes up space. All matter has **mass**. Mass is the amount of material that something has. Matter can be sorted into three main **states**, or forms—solids, liquids, and gases.

Air is a gas that is used to pump up tires.

Gasoline is a liquid fuel that makes vehicles move. Sometimes the name is shortened to "gas." But it is not the same as the state of matter known as gas.

It is a gas!

Did you breathe in a gas today? If you are alive, then the answer is yes! Air is an invisible gas. It flows in and out of your lungs every time you breathe.

Talking about matter

Each state of matter has different **properties**. Properties are ways to describe how something looks, feels, tastes, or smells. A property is something that makes one thing different from other things.

Gas

A gas is a type of matter that moves easily. It spreads out evenly to fill the space it is in. It does not have its own shape. It takes the shape of any container it is put into.

Liquid

A liquid is a type of matter that moves or flows. It can be poured. It does not have its own shape. It takes the shape of any container it is put into.

Solid

A solid is a type of matter that keeps its shape. It does not change shape when placed in different containers.

What do you think?

Can you find all three states of matter here?

7

Properties of a gas

Sometimes you cannot see a gas. But a gas can have other properties that tell you it is there. Wind is fast moving air. You can feel it on your face on a windy day. Even though you cannot see the wind, you can feel it.

You can see the air move flags on a windy day.

The smoke from a campfire is a mix of gases and other material. Sometimes you can see it. Breathe in through your nose, and you can smell it. **Odor**, or smell, is a property of some gases.

Perfume is a mix of liquid and gas. When perfume is sprayed, the gas is carried through the air by water droplets that evaporate leaving the odor of the gas.

What do you

Ask a parent to take a bottle of perfume with you into a small room and close the door. Have your parent spray a bit from the bottle on one side of the room while you stand on the far side of the room. How long does it take before you can smell the perfume? Does the smell grow stronger as it spreads throughout the room?

9

Taking up space

A gas takes up space. Even though you cannot see some gases, they are still there. You can see this when you blow up a balloon. You fill the balloon with the air from inside your lungs.

No shape of its own

A gas does not have its own shape. It spreads out to take the shape of the container it is in. Air that you breathe in takes the shape of your lungs. The air you breathe out takes the shape of the room you are in.

Put a straw in a glass and fill it to the very top with water. Blow air through the straw into the water. What does air inside the water look like? How do you know air takes up space in the water? (Hint: What happens to the water when air is blown into it?)

Measuring gas

You might think that because you cannot see gas it does not weigh anything—but it does! A gas is made up of tiny **particles**, or pieces, we cannot see with our eyes. These particles give gas its mass and weight.

What do you think?

Gases are light. Helium and air are both gases, but helium is lighter than air. If you fill one balloon with helium and another with air, the helium balloon floats upward while the air-filled balloon sinks. Why do you think the helium-filled balloon floats in the air?

Fill it up!

A gas has no **volume** of its own. Volume is the amount of space matter takes up. A gas changes its shape to fill any size container. So the volume of a gas is the same as the volume of its container. When a gas is moved to a new container, its volume changes to the new container's volume.

13

Changing states

Most matter stays in one state at **room temperature**. A solid stays a solid. A liquid stays a liquid. A gas stays a gas. All matter stays the same unless you do something to change it. A **physical change** is when matter changes the way it looks.

Vapor is another word for gas. Steam, or water vapor, is a gas that you can sometimes see. When it spreads out to fill an entire room, however, you cannot see it anymore.

This kitchen is filled with water vapor that you cannot see.

Most matter changes from one state to another when you add or take away energy. Heat is a type of energy that changes matter. Matter can change states when its temperature is changed. After being changed, some types of matter, such as water, can even be changed back to its first state.

What do you think?

Pour water into an ice cube tray. Put the tray into the freezer and let it freeze. The liquid water will change states and became a solid. Now, take the tray out of the freezer and leave it in the hot sun. What happens to the solid water?

From a liquid to a gas

Some liquids change to a gas or vapor when heat is added to them. When a liquid changes to a gas, we say it evaporates. Can you find the word "vapor" in evaporation?

Steam is a gas

An adult can add heat to a pot of liquid water by turning on the stove burner underneath. Water boils when its temperature reaches 212 degrees Fahrenheit (100 degrees Celsius). This temperature is called the **boiling point**. The water changes from a liquid into a gas that rises from the pot. This gas, or water vapor, in the air is called steam.

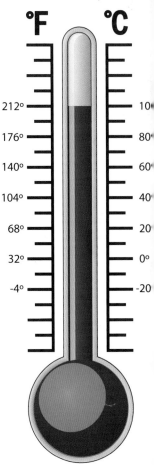

°F   °C

212° — 10
176° — 80
140° — 60
104° — 40
68° — 20
32° — 0°
-4° — -20

What do you think?

After it rains, you see puddles on the ground. When the day turns sunny, the puddles disappear. What makes the water in the puddles disappear?

From a gas to a liquid

Some gases change states when they are cooled. To cool a gas, you take heat away from it. A gas can change into a liquid when it is cooled. When a gas changes to a liquid, we say it **condenses**.

Invisible water vapor goes through a physical change when it cools and becomes a cloud you can see.

Too cool!

Water vapor is a gas that rises up in the air. On Earth, you cannot see the water vapor going up. The air is colder the higher up you go. The colder temperature condenses the water vapor, or changes it into liquid water droplets. The puffy clouds you can see in the sky are made up of these water droplets.

What do you think?

When you breathe out on a warm day, you cannot see your breath. Why do think you can see your breath in a little white puff when you breathe out on a very cold day?

Glass empty or full?

Even when a glass is empty, it is still full—of air! This activity shows that a gas takes up space in a container even when you cannot see it.

What you will need:

a drinking glass

a paper towel

a sink or glass bowl filled with water

What to do:

1 Crumple up the paper towel and push it to the bottom of the drinking glass so that it stays inside.

2 Turn the glass upside down so that the open part is facing downward. The paper towel should stay at the bottom of the glass and not fall out.

3 Hold the upside-down glass straight up and down over the water and push it down flat to the bottom of the bowl. Make sure the open part of the glass does not tilt.

4 Now pull the glass up out of the water, still holding it straight up and down. Pull the paper towel out of the glass.

What do you think?

Why is the paper towel still dry?

Answer: The paper towel is dry because the glass was filled with both the paper towel and air. When the glass was pushed into the water, the air filled the rest of the glass up so there was no room for the water to seep into the glass!

What can you build with gas?

Dip a wand in liquid soap. Move it through the air. The liquid soap surrounds the air, which is a gas, to make a bubble. You can also make air bubbles in a liquid by sticking a straw into it and blowing. The bubbles rise and pop at the surface.

A hot-air balloon is a vehicle that travels through the air. The balloon is also filled with air inside. The air inside the balloon is warmed by a fuel called propane gas. Warm air always rises. The warm air takes the balloon and its basket up with it.

A blimp is a large airship filled with helium gas. Helium gas is lighter than air, so the airship floats in the sky. Large engines move it forward from one place to another.

Learning more

Books

Amazing Materials (Amazing Science series)
by Sally Hewitt, Crabtree Publishing, 2008.

Changing Materials (Working with Materials series)
by Chris Oxlade, Crabtree Publishing, 2008.

Websites

www.harcourtschool.com/activity/states_of_matter
Find out how particles in a solid, a liquid, or a gas behave
under a virtual microscope on this website.

http://e-learningforkids.org/Courses/EN/S0602/index.html
Mr. Beaker explains the three main states of matter, and how
and why they change, on this fun and interactive website.

http://www.sciencekids.co.nz/gamesactivities/gases.html
Enjoy these fun, interactive science activities that allow you to
experiment with changing states of matter.

Glossary

Note: Some boldfaced words are defined where they appear in the book.

boiling point [BOY-ling point] *noun*
The temperature at which a liquid changes from a liquid to a gas

condense [kun-DENS] *verb* To bring closer together

evaporate [ih-VAP-uh-reyt] *verb*
To change from a liquid into a gas

odor [O-der] *adjective* The smell that something gives off

physical change [FIZ-i-kel CHAYNJ]
adjective and noun A change in the way matter looks

property [PROP-er-tee] *noun*
A special quality or attribute that a kind of matter has.

room temperature [RUME TEMP-er-a-chur] *adjective*
Something that is the same temperature as the room it is in

*A noun is a person, place, or thing. A verb is an action word that tells you what someone or something does.
An adjective is a word that tells you what something is like.*

Index